BEFORE
I
FAILED

Tomas Veres

FIRST EDITION
Cover design: Tomas Veres
Translation: Miriam Oravcova
Editor: Tatran English Services, LLC.

www.tomasveres.com

instagram/tomasveres_

goodreads.com/tomasveres

ISBN 978-80-570-0378-6

To my heroes David Wakeman and Frederik Van Lierde.

You gave me the reason to continue with what I love
during the times when I hated it the most.
God bless you.

I love to eat bananas, drink freshwater and
gazing up at the shining stars in the night sky.

This doesn't mean that you should also love eating
bananas, drinking freshwater and gazing up
at the shining stars in the night sky.

Don't be me, be you.

Don't be fake, be original.

"**P**lease, Sir, come down from the ledge. Don't do anything *stupid. People are waiting for you at home who care about you. They need you. Please, come down.*"

"Why, man? Why should I listen to you?

I have no reason to get down. I have no one to go back to. I lost everything. I lost everything I ever cared about.

My clothes, my garage, my safe, crammed with bright and shiny objects. My heart is empty. You can't find anything there.

Only emptiness. Darkness."

"You can always do something about it. You can always fix what you've ruined. You can always change your life. This is not the solution to your problems. Open your heart. Share your worries about your life. I'm here for you. I want to help you. If talking is what will help you, please talk to me."

"Everything happened so fast. I had such a perfect life. Everything was perfect. I had everything.

A loving fiancé, success, money, recognition, my own studio. I only have material things now. Only these material things haven't left me.

I feel lonely as fuck!"

"What happened? What caused all these problems? What made you commit to such an act?"

"Me. I did it on my own!

A few years ago I opened my own small architectural studio here in Los Angeles. It was just a tiny office and me on Hollywood Blvd."

"Close to the Mosaic Church?"

"Yes, near the Mosaic Church."

Companies, developers from around the world wanted to work with me. I even designed this very hotel in my studio. Before I opened my own studio, I went through hell. You can not imagine the things I had to face to get away from the dirt I was living in. After I opened my studio, I lived my life as if I were in paradise. I had everything I wanted. At least I thought I had everything I wanted.

Every day I woke up at 6 am. I brushed my teeth. I ate five sunny-side-up eggs with a slice of whole grain bread. Meditation, visualization, affirmation, reading a book – my own "hour of growth." I took my fiancé Sara to her work about 4 minutes away from our house. Then I started to do what I was extraordinary at. Drawing.

It didn't matter whether it was a hotel, a mansion or a skyscraper. With my experience, with my talent, I always managed to do something. Every night, after I finished my drawings of buildings, I went running on the beach. Thanks to this running, I got everything harmful out of my head, away from my mind. With a clear mind, I could spend the rest of the day with the most important person in my life: Sara.

That's how a normal day went for a few years. Of course, there were exceptions when we were spending time with friends, but most of all, I had so much work that I was not in the mood or I had no time to go out and meet up with other people. What I was doing, the life I was living, it fulfilled me. Even when I had a shitload of money, I did not spend it. I didn't need it. I was happy with being average.

An average house.

Average car.

Average clothes.

I didn't even have the time to think about some other house than the one I owned, other clothes than the ones I was wearing. Some different car than the one I was driving. With what I owned, I fit perfectly into our neighborhood.

Ordinary things, owned by an extraordinary person, right?

Right!

Everything changed when, on one Monday morning, this confident guy came to my studio with an unusual demand. Nobody had ever asked me this before. Most of my clients did not have a clear idea of how the design of their building would eventually look like. This guy had nothing in common with the others. I hadn't even made up my mind on whether I would draw his megayacht or not, and he had already given me a $90,000 check.

"Are your skilled hands capable of doing such a remarkable job?" he asked me.

"Of course, my hands are capable of doing whatever my clients want." That was my answer.

I took it as a challenge.

Only a few minutes after the arrival of this unknown guy into my studio, I had accepted a contract that meant a shift forward for my business if I exceeded my client's expectations – or the end of my business in the case of my client's dissatisfaction. As I think about it now, for the first time after I had finally succeeded, I took a risk.

As soon as I put the $90,000 check into my safe, my phone rang. An unknown number. Maybe a potential client, I thought. I picked it up. Then I heard the same voice of the guy who had been standing right in front of me in my studio a few minutes ago. Marion, the man wanting the megayacht, asked me to go out to the front of my studio. I put the phone on the table, I finished my yerba mate, and without answering the question in my head of why he wanted to meet me outside my studio, I went out. The sun's rays immediately blinded my eyes, tired after looking into my notebook for too long. While my eyes fought with the sun, my ears enjoyed the sweet sound of exotic cars driving by on the street in front of my studio. I thought they were some wealthy young guys with a good mood trying to impress me. I was wrong.

There were no rich guys in the street trying to impress me as they drove by. Marion and his friends were the ones sitting in those cars, trying to impress me. And I tell you, they did a great job. I felt like a little kid in Disney Land.

From a light blue car marked with a gold 23 sticker, Marion stepped out. This time he wore another watch on his wrist.

Crazy, right ?!

It had not even been 10 minutes and the guy had already exchanged his watch for another. Even women don't have the need to change their clothes so often. A strong smell wafted over from him. The ocean air wasn't strong enough to fight the aroma of his cologne.

Nice to see you again, "Mr. Pencil," he remarked wittily.

Then he insisted on going to see his luxury mansion in Bel Air, which he told me cost 1000 bitcoins. I tried to explain to him that behind me was a studio in which unfinished work was waiting for me. Something I needed to work on with an ASAP post-it note on top of it.

I don't know if it was the exotic cars or his strong personality, but I finally accepted his invitation to visit his luxury mansion. Anyhow, an hour without work wouldn't kill me. I am my own boss, I decide what I do. With these words, I silenced the remorse coming from my conscience. By the way, it was actually the first time I had interrupted my work in the studio. Even on the wedding day of my friend John's daughter, I did not leave my studio. I went back to the studio to grab my phone and locked the security door. Then I did a weird thing, according to most people. I got in the car, an expensive car mind you, of a strange guy, someone I had only known since that morning.

When I jumped into Marion's car, my mind was flying in the clouds. I felt so different. Different than when I was driving my 8-year-old Toyota Auris.

Leather with contrasting embroidery.

The music coming out of the speakers right from a G-Eazy concert.

The sound of the engine, I can not even describe it.

It simply was awesome.

At high speeds, we raced down Sunset Boulevard straight to his luxury mansion in Bel Air. Pure adrenaline pumped through my veins. At every crossroads with a red traffic light, we were the ones everybody looked at. We were the center of attention like some stars from a TV show. Girls, all the pretty ones, couldn't take their eyes off us. All the guys, young and old alike, walking along the sidewalk were filming us on their smartphones.

The road I had traveled at least a thousand times in my life like an invisible breeze changed on that day into a road that I drove down like a shining star in the dark night sky.

The same city, the same road, but different people, different car – an entirely different experience.

As I sat in that huge leather seat, from the passenger window I looked out at the same world around me with a completely different look in my eyes.

When we arrived at Marion's mansion, I couldn't believe my own eyes. I had designed this luxury mansion, bought for 1000 bitcoins, when I worked back at my old architectural firm. In the architectural firm where I had started as an ordinary trainee. Unbelievable.

"Do you recognize this building?" he asked me with a wide smile on his face.

"How... How did you know?"

"Tom, don't be so modest! Look at yourself! You are one of the best, most wanted architects in the entire United States of America. My father had to pay $40,000 for an ad in a magazine that regularly features you and your buildings on the cover.

For free. In each edition."

After a few words of praise, I got the opportunity to know my own creation and see it with my own eyes. Marion continued to praise me, while my inner voice spoke to me: "Well there Tom! You drew hundreds of more beautiful mansions than this."

I peeked into each room. I'm gonna tell you that guy had fucking good taste. The furniture, carpets, marble, sculptures, paintings. Everything went together so perfectly. Everything looked so perfect. Everything looked so luxurious. Even the girls swimming in the huge pool, looked so luxurious and so perfect. Every single girl I would be willing to invite for a date if I hadn't met Sara.

The luxury mansion, garage full of foreign cars in various color, magnificent creatures in the pool, and at the dock a soon to arrive megayacht.

"**M**arion, how did you do it? Do you own a software company, or something like that?" I asked him out of curiosity.

"Are you kidding me ?! I' m not one of those kids sitting behind a computer for 22 hours typing unknown code on the keyboard! I'm one of those kids who make good money on technology made by kids sitting 22 hours a day on the computer writing weird code on their keyboards.

I'm an influencer. An Instagram influencer.

Let me tell you, it's a huge business. All the world's best companies pay me hundreds of thousands of dollars for silly photos of their stupid things.

I call it easy money, they call it advertising.

Take a look! This fashion brand paid me almost $200,000 to wear their terrible looking t-shirt in a 30 second video ..."

"How many pieces did the fashion brand sell while they collaborated with you?" I needed to know, so I asked him.

"Honestly, I don't know! And I don't care. Maybe they earned another $200,000 because of me, or they lost $200,000. I don't care!

I have a better question for you, Tom. What are you doing tonight? Hmm..."

I tried to find an appropriate answer in my head. But I sadly appreciated my evening program, probably watching a movie with Sara in bed. The usual.

"I'll spend tonight in the company of my lovely fiancé Sara" was my answer.

"Really? That's how the best architects spend their Monday nights? Dude! Tonight I'll show you how I spend each night from Monday to Sunday. I promise you won't be bored. Bring your girl too, she won't be the only girl at that party. You know, tonight, there will be a crowd of people, especially girls around our age, Tom."

If I refused his invitation, I would look like a loser. Maybe I should ask Sara if she would agree, but this time I made up my mind for the both of us. No Deadpool 2 today, as Sara had suggested earlier in a text. This evening, a breath of fresh air, surrounded by real human beings. Like in the old days with John's family.

6:41.
Sitting on a cracked brown leather armchair, looking at the love of my life, just arriving. I'm thinking about telling her about a party that starts in less than 2 hours. Should I say that right now? Or should I tell her as a surprise just before the party starts? What if she doesn't want to go? What will Marion think about me? If I don't show up, despite my promise, without saying anything directly to his face?

With the sound of Sara's creamy stilettos, the scent of Sara's vanilla perfume, my thoughts got lost. It was now or never. As soon as she kissed me, as soon as she embraced me, I shared with her the fact that we would be going to a party for two hours in my new friend's luxury mansion. In Bel Air.

As I expected, Sara was not interested in going to the party. I was naïve, hoping for another answer. She had a hard day at work, and she was not in the mood and didn't have the energy to be in the company of other people for another hour. I tried to talk to her several times and change her mind. It's going to be better for both of us to go out, to get to know new people, to have fun. Let's have fun, we deserve it. But I got the same answer as before.

I didn't have a choice. I had to get ready to watch boring Deadpool 2, with the fact that my new client today had really made an impression on me – while I was not keeping my promise to him, because I would be a no-show to his party thanks to my beloved, but at the same time tired, fiancé.

Maybe it was the tone of my voice, or the expression on my face, that revealed my feelings to Sara, disappointed by her decision not to go to the party. Hiding my feelings never was one of my stronger characteristics.

8:27. Sara looked directly into my eyes and said:

"I'd like to go there with you. I'm sure we'd have a lot of fun. Today, at work, it took all my energy. Now I'm going to lie in bed, and you go to that party in Bel Air." She hugged me and left for bed.

No disappointment, no promise-breaking. I felt as great as I had that morning. As fast as I could, I put on some khaki trousers, a white shirt and shouted "I love you, honey!" A minute later I sat behind the steering wheel in my Toyota on my way to Marion. Sara had literally saved my reputation. My promise had been kept. I made it on time.

Big black men in suits welcomed me at the entrance gate. I rolled down the window. That loud music sounded deafening to *me*. *"If you need something or you have a problem, we are here for you, Mr. Seed."*

It was my first time meeting such nice and polite bouncers… I remembered back to the times when bouncers would "welcome" me back in New York. But those guys didn't have such nice suits or such a nice approach to me.

Behind the huge entrance gate, I hardly found any places to park my car. All these luxury cars were shiny and polished. Even from a distance, I noticed how shiny they were. Only my old Auris looked like a renegade among them. Like the car belonging to the gardener of that luxury mansion. Immediately as I stepped out, a young woman in a lacy swimsuit handed me a crystal champagne glass. I took the glass of champagne out of politeness. Nothing more. You know, I had never drank a drop of alcohol in my life, I knew very well what this can do to people and their families. Yet here I was, accompanied by an attractive blonde into a world unrecognizable by me. Around me, at least 50 people were dancing to the rhythm of electro music. The DJ was up on a stage close to the pool. Tables full of golden bottles with champagne. I did not see any people there without a look joy on their faces, sparkles in their eyes.

I stood there with my mouth wide open. Literally! I could not believe what I was seeing. I had never even seen a party like this in any movie. In a moment, when I was least expecting it, Marion came up to me from behind.

I barely had the chance to say hello to him before his companions were bringing me inside the luxury mansion. To the kitchen. Of course, he was moaning about my clothes. He thought I dressed myself like I was going to the library to study chemistry.

I stood there surrounded by seven girls. The seven most beautiful girls I had ever seen in my life. A concrete wall separated us from the other party guests. The kitchen had become a VIP zone. Only me, Marion and the seven angels. One of the angels brought a bottle of wine from the cellar. Red wine.

On the marble counter she placed 9 glasses.

Into each of them, she poured the French red wine. Then everyone picked up one glass. Except for me. I'm telling you this embarrassing situation, one that I had not experienced for a long time. I felt horrible.

They looked at me like I was an alien.

The disturbing silence was interrupted by Marion's sarcastic remark:

"What's going on, Tom? No way you are abstinent..."

Another awkward situation ahead of me. I had to answer his question. "Right, Marion, I'm clean!"

Without thinking about my answer, everyone around me started to laugh. All but me. All my life, I was so proud of myself that I had not drunk a drop of alcohol until this evening. But my pride was replaced by shame. "Do not be so hard on yourself, Tom! Live a little!" my inner voice shouted.

Without any useless speech, with no shame, I took a glass from the marble countertop and drank it all. Their laughter was replaced with applause. They encouraged me to drink another glass. When I finished the second glass of red wine, they kept going. Still encouraging me, another one, another one.

Of course I listened to them. I drank a whole bottle of wine. No sentiments, no conscience, no dignity. On the contrary, I was amazed. I did not understand how I could ever abstain from drinking. I did not understand how I could do this to myself, not to experience those amazing feelings associated with drinking alcohol.

The more alcohol in my veins, the fewer restrictions in my head. Without fear of what people would think of me, without any hesitation, I stripped off my sweaty white shirt, I grabbed the hand of a girl with black hair standing right next to me, and took her with me to jump right into the pool. My spontaneous deed inspired many other girls dancing by the pool. Even in my wildest dreams, I would never had pictured the party I was actually living through. Monday night and I was swimming in a pool entirely drunk, half-naked in the middle of a bunch of half-naked girls touching my body. Sara, at home, was asleep, tired from work, while I was having the best night of my life. And all thanks to Marion, who had visited me in my studio earlier that day with a request to design a megayacht.

Tuesday, 11:19 am. I woke up at home in my bed with a massive headache. I had no clue how I got from Bel Air to my home. I remember almost everything that had happened the previous night, I just couldn't remember how I got myself home. Even my car was safe in front of the garage. No damage.

The breakfast that Sara prepared before she left for work without my escort I had to throw in the trash. My stomach was unable to accept any food. My body needed only one single thing: water. A lot of water.

For almost 2 years, all my days had looked the same. Of course there were some exceptions, but it was not comparable to what I had live through the previous day. That morning, or really the afternoon, after that party had a completely different vibe than usual. No breakfast, no meditation, no book, no driving Sara to work. Also, the designs of the buildings I had been working were just laying on the table in my studio. It took me some time to start drawing. I would not have done it without a taking cold shower first. When I finally decided to draw a new skyscraper to be built in Manila, I found a paper with the design of Marion's megayacht. I drew it up shortly after he had visited my studio yesterday. Even when my eyes looked at the paper with the megayacht proposal, my mind was imagining the life of the owner of that megayacht.

Marion, who came into my life only a day ago, had already made such a strong impression on me. I literally set up an Instagram account only to follow his amazing life captured in his many photos. The most recent photo added to his profile was amusingly great. He had taken the picture as I swam in the pool with the group of girls shortly after my first jump. Marion's friends were also tagged in it. The photo had more than 70,000 likes and thousands of comments.

Some girls had written in the comments:

"Oh, sweetheart"

"Cute face looks like he works out"

"I could imagine more than just an innocent swim in the pool"

"Wow, he knows how to enjoy life"

Suddenly my appearance, unappreciated by my fiancé, had unknown women admiring it.

I thought the picture was the best of all the pictures Marion had ever added to his Instagram account. Unfortunately, I was wrong. Marion had added hundreds and hundreds of similar photos. And most captured many more crazier, much more exciting moments, which I was not part of.

That day, I could no longer sat down at the table in my studio. I was not in the mood to do anything but to answer the questions bouncing around in my head. Just think of the life I was living. I was looking for some day, some moment when I could enjoy my life like I had at the party. I could have spent hours going through my memories – weeks, months – but I still found nothing to compare it to. Absolutely nothing.

I realized that my whole life was like some old grandfather right before his death.

No excitement.
No partying.
No adventures.
No adrenaline.
No experiences.
No memories of friends.
No risks.

I would have nothing to talk about to my future grandchildren, only if they would like to hear stories about how I was sitting in my studio every day alone, with a pencil, notebook, and paper.

You know, this was true even though I officially belonged to the group of successful individuals with proven results.

Even though I had a shitload of money.

Even though I could have anything, I lived a poor life.

Once, my friend John had told me that I'm an extraordinary person.

Is this how life should be for an extraordinary person? An average life?

A poor life? Really?

I knew at least 20 guys who did not even have a fraction of what I had, who did not reach a fraction of what I had achieved, and despite all that, they were living rich lives unlike me.

They drove better cars than I did.

They wore better clothes than I wore.

They lived in better homes than I did.

I had the same right to this lifestyle, but I didn't go for it. What a shame, to see the young 18-year-old clerk from Walmart driving a brand new BMW for $42,000 while I was driving ...

"What had happened to me that I allowed myself to live such an average, poor life?" I asked myself.

In my life, I realized I had followed this rule:

I only have one life to live, so why should I risk it.

I did not eat food like pizza or ice cream because I did not want to feed my body with waste that would hurt me. I didn't drive quickly because I did not want to get in an accident or kill myself.

I went to sleep around 10 because I did not want to sleep fewer hours than would be good for my health.

I did not drink alcohol because I saw in my childhood what can be done by people who drank too much.

I did not celebrate, because I thought it was a waste of my precious time.

I did not spend my money on things, experiences, because I had to go through hell to achieve them and I did not want to lose anything.

Whenever I was able to spend time with other people, I was one of the weird ones. I always ate some different foods than them, I drank different drinks, I did some different things, I talked about different topics.

I created a barrier between them and me.

I had a dull, secure life in my house, protected from the outbursts of the outside world. You know I thought I was hiding in a deep cave like a bear. Only work, sleep, books, meditation, running, watching fucking boring movies with Sara.

Every day, every week, every month.

Why should I live such a mean, poor life when I was rich?

Why should I leave my life in one place when I had the money to live my life, to spend my life, in any part of the world?

Why couldn't I use my hard-earned money?

Why should I be modest when I did not have to be?
Why, when people do weird things, could not I do weird things as well?

That night, in the evening when Sara returned home from work, she asked how the party was after I came back home the next day.

For a moment I was thinking what to say, then

I decided to tell her only the parts I had to say. We had a little fun. A little evening with the guys. Nothing more. The whole story I kept for myself due for obvious reasons. She did not have a clue what happened there. I suggested that we go to a restaurant on the beach like we used to do in the past. Get out of that boring stereotype. She made some excuses due to her work again. How tired she was, how much work had to be done, how hard she is working to get her promotion. How she would like to go out with me, but, but…

I told her it was fine, even when it was not fine. She was caught in the same trap as I was.

We both lived for work instead of working for a living. We had become slaves of our own lives.

We preferred to be sure instead of spontaneity.

We killed the small child inside us, comfort was satisfying to us.

Comfort had limited us.

When we crawled into bed, Sara was sleeping while I was tossing and turning from one side to another. I could not sleep. My thoughts were stronger than my need for 8 hours of healthy sleep. In my head, I rewatched the party from the previous night. I tried to forget it. I did not think of anything else. On my phone, I checked emails from my clients. It helped me to think of something else, just like the previous night. Then I received an email. Instant notification: Marion had tagged me in his video.

My heart was jumping like crazy with adrenaline pumping in my veins. I was so excited and so scared. Marion had uploaded a video from another party. This time in Ibiza with the commentar*y: "You should be here with us, my brother @iamtomseed."*

After seeing the video, I did not feel jealousy or hatred. Regret, that was what I felt. I almost cried. I was so eager to be there with them in Ibiza, to be one of all the young people bursting with joy on their faces. Living life to the max, not with my hand on the brakes.

Filling your life, not just your wallet.

One look at my surroundings said it all. A tired fiancé sleeping close to me. I hardly remembered one day when we had some adventure, excitement, or something special that I would remember forever. Our relationship had become a race. Who will achieve more with our work?

Nothing else.

The romance at the beginning of our relationship had now disappeared. What we were connected with at the beginning was splitting us now.

Sara was determined to sacrifice her own life for work, I'm determined to sacrifice something for my own life. I was not able to take my eyes off Instagram until morning. I looked at Marion's photos, photos of his friends and pictures of other people. All of them had done so many interesting things and me?

I was working every single day in my studio on the buildings where these people are now living their spirited lives. I could create something for other people. Give them a living space. And I was unable to create the same place for my own life.

In that photo in the pool, I looked happy. Happier than usual. A smile on my face, a sparkle in my eyes. I looked different in the pictures with Sara in our living room. With a different expression on my face, without a sincere smile, but no sparkles in the eyes.

With dark circles under my eyes, with the mess in my head, with desire in my heart, I sat down behind the desk in my studio, where I finished the last details on the Manila skyscraper. For two fucking months I had worked day by day on that skyscraper.

No breaks.

No vacation.

No social life.

In other words, I spent more time with a pencil than with a human being. I could not live this life anymore.

If this is called "life" at all.

"So what did you decide to do with the life that you were living so far?"

"First I evaluated what I needed to change in my life. After a brief time thinking, I came to the conclusion that I had to change my whole life."

"How did you make that decision, to change your life?"

"It was not that difficult to make this decision.

I felt that I was not living the life I should live. I saw firsthand that I was living the life I should be living. Everything around me, everything in me screamed: you deserve more than just this!"

Even though I had succeeded, even though I had a tremendous amount of money in my bank account, even though I belonged among the best architects in the United States, I did not feel like I was the successful, rich and best architect in the USA. Yes, I knew that what I was doing, I was extraordinary at it. But it made no sense for me to live such an ordinary life. I had everything I needed to live an extraordinary life. Not just to be an extraordinary person. I hid it deep in my mind, like some mystery. Without a willingness to share my feelings, successes, dreams, or opinions with the outside world. About my inner me.

I lived in a house that was not equal to my success, my property, my personality.

I drove a car that did not match my success, my property, my personality.

Just like I had spent my days in a way that didn't match my success, my property, my personality.

The clothes I wore did not match my success, my property, my personality.

It had nothing to do with modesty. It was caused by my own decision to live my life deep below my level. I was satisfied with the simplicity. In those years I had developed my own inner world. I was working on my mind and soul. Meditation, visualization, affirmation. Yes, it had helped me enough. I just forgot to pay attention to the other things. The outside world. The outside world I had been neglecting for years. I did not pay any attention to it, because my eyes were looking into me – not around me, not in front of me. I did not want to look anymore at all these ordinary guys like I was one of them. It took too long. I had looked like one of them for too long. I had been one of them for too long.

If Marion would not have come into my studio that Monday morning to ask me to draw the blueprints for his megayacht, if I did not attend his party that evening, I'm afraid I would never realize how poor the life I was living.

You know.

Marion was 28, exactly like I was.

Marion was successful, exactly like I was.

Marion lived in Los Angeles, exactly like I did.

Marion had a lot of money, exactly like I had.

This connected us.

I fell asleep every evening beside the same woman, while Marion spent every night with a different girl.

I lived in a cheap house designed by some of unknown architect, while Marion lived in a luxury mansion designed by me.

I was known in the architect community, Marion was known all over the world.

I drove an ugly car, while Marion rode a gorgeous, exotic supercar.

I wore clothes worth just a couple of dollars, while Marion wore clothes worth a thousand dollars.

I had saved my money, while Marion spent his money.

Two guys the same age, living in the same city with a similar amount of money in their bank accounts, only with a totally different lifestyle. Without a doubt, my approach to life had cost me a great deal. Not just memories, but also my dignity.

If only...

That's why I chose to pursue a different lifestyle, the same lifestyle as Marion had.

I only have one life to live, so damnit I'm gonna enjoy it. I'm not going to take my money with me to the grave. What doesn't kill me makes me stronger. Better to die going for a crazy ride in a crazy car than sitting on the sofa and watching a boring movie.

I briefly called all my clients. I told them the terms of submission for the designs of their buildings that we had previously agreed upon would not be delivered on time. I did not explain to them why or what was happening. I had only a brief answer to this, and I would say clearly: "a lot of things are going on in my architectural studio." Maybe each client was a little disappointed and surprised. But in each case, they agreed with the proposals being delayed. No clients opted to cancel their collaboration with me. I had postponed all the agreed projects, except for one: the draft of the megayacht for my new friend, Marion. Again, I started to take risks like I had in the past, and let me tell you I was loving it.

"What changes did you intend to make when you postponed all the projects?"

Big changes. I was not just planning. I immediately implemented them. In less than 30 minutes since I thought up the idea, I made it happen. I posted on LinkedIn that I was looking for sophisticated architects that would like to get the chance to achieve something big. In less than 30 minutes, I had made the necessary changes that could take me to the next level. Why should I be satisfied with a local architectural studio when I had the talent, money, experience, and knowledge to build an international architecture company?

Yes, in my little studio, I was my own boss, but I was also the only slave of my studio. That's why I spent so much time locked between those four walls with a pencil in my hand. Nobody else besides me could finish the building designs. I did not have any people who would do it instead of me. If I kept going on like this, my life would look the same as before. I could not let this happen in any way.

2 hours after adding my post to LinkedIn, I was approached by 21 architects. Each one I immediately invited to interview at my studio. 17 of them showed up in front of the door to the studio, standing in a row. Within a couple of minutes, after a strict selection process, three of them

were already sitting on chairs behind the table, waiting for a short training.

They made it perfect. I felt incredibly well.

My confidence was immediately through the roof. What would have previously taken months or years, now that I dared to take the risk on that day, I could do in less than 3 hours. I did not stop just by recruiting a new staff. I went on and on. I called my clients who I had called in the morning. This time I had very nice news for them. The delayed projects would be finished without any delays. Even much earlier than we had agreed. And all thanks to my 3 new employees, willing to work hard for me, long hours every day. Before it took me about 2 months to design one skyscraper to the last detail. 2 months of hard work, at least 12 hours a day of hard work from Monday to Sunday.

Week by week.

Step by step.

In other words, my studio was able to design one skyscraper in about two months.

Nothing more.

In one year I proposed six skyscrapers. Thanks to my three newly recruited employees, my studio was able to design at least three skyscrapers every two months, three times more than before.

Eighteen skyscrapers in one year.

More projects, more clients, more money.

No matter how hard I thought, I was not able to find any disadvantages to my plan.

Only benefits.

I will no longer have to be locked in my studio between those four walls, my staff would do it for me.

I will not be that small fish in the pond anymore, I would now be the shark in the ocean.

I will no longer earn $400,000 a year, my staff would help me make millions and millions of dollars each year.

I will no longer be known only in the United States, people would know the name Tom Seed all over the world.

I will no longer celebrate my success in my head, all my successes would be celebrated in the world around me.

What would have taken 5, 10, 15 years or more to achieve, I could achieve in one year thanks to hiring other people.

I will no longer work for myself, other people would work for me.

I will no longer be my own great boss, now I would be the boss of someone else.

I will no longer be the owner of a small architectural studio, I would be the owner of an architectural business.

"**W**hy *did you choose those three job applicants? What distinguished them from the other 14?*"

The same story. We were connected by the same story. They also come from dirt like me. They also fought for their lives, before they found out who they were and what they are extraordinary at, like me.

The other applicants came from good families, with property, with money. If I accepted one of them, I am sure they would not be willing to sacrifice something for my business. To give up something nice for me. You know, they did not need to be the best, they did not have to fight for a better life. They lived a better life thanks to their parents. However, those three people I hired knew very well that no one would give them anything for free, that they would not get anything for free anywhere. Only hard work would bring them something in return. I gave them a place to fulfill their dreams, their potential. In return for this, I demanded hard work from them.

Every day, long hours.

Week by week.

Month by month.

Devoted to my job, to the projects of my company.

I knew exactly how to handle them.

I knew exactly how to motivate them.

I knew exactly what words I should tell them.

Because I was the same as them. I did not need a wise book for this.

I just had it in myself.

On one day, one decision ended up changing my life. Those days when I spent the entire day in the studio to work on the design of a building were over. I found somebody to do it for me. Now I had to think of what I would do with the free time I had. How to spend the 12 hours of free time I did not have before.

Sleeping, movies, or video games were not even to be discussed. I took inspiration from Marion.

I called him and asked if we could meet.

I was lucky. He had just come back from Miami so I could come over to his mansion. When I came to the entrance gate decorated with a gold dollar, a tall guy with the camera was filming Marion talking about something. I would have to spend my precious time just guessing what the hell that guy was doing, so I got out of the car and quietly approached the guy with the camera observing what was going on. Surprisingly, Marion was not giving some pep talk or sharing life-changing words.

Marion talked about his soon-to-be party at a local club where he could personally meet his fans, especially the girls from his fan club. That party was supposed to take place on Friday that week. The cameraman finished his job, looked over the results, and then he left. As expected, I received an invitation to join the party together with Sara. Not as ordinary guests, but as VIP guests. Of course I accepted it without any hesitation. Only a fool would refuse it.

Two glasses of French wine, from 1920, helped me to lose my "silence."

"Marion, I've made such big changes today. Today, I have proven some amazing things to myself. Without you I could not have done it, you gave me the motivation, gave me an example of how to live a real life. In my studio, I made specific changes.

Big changes.

I am no longer just my own boss. Now I am the boss of someone else – my three new employees, willing to work hard. I came here to ask you for advice on how to take my life even further. Now that I don't have to be locked in my studio, I have some free time. This time I would like to take fully for myself. To enjoy these 12 hours, not to miss out during these 12 hours. You know how to live your life 100 percent. Tell me what to do with my free time.

How should I use it?"

"It's simple. Your real life is outside your comfort zone, outside of your house, outside of your sofa, outside of your studio.

If you start to spend more time outside these comfortable prisons, you will start to live.

Believe me, once you start, you will no longer need to be shut down in your house or in your studio.

A place that gives you a sense of home, safety, warmth takes from you the feeling of a real-life experience. When you die, you are going to be locked in a wooden coffin, so why, when you come home, should you lock yourself in your wooden house, between four shitty walls, just like a corpse.

Enjoy your life as long as your body can. Because the time will come when you will not be able to, the time will come when your body will not be able to. Don't look at how other people live their lives. Let other people look at you as you live your own life!"

Marion was right. Since I became successful, I stopped living. That time in New York, or when I came to Los Angeles, I was living my life.

And when I lived on the streets as a homeless guy, even when I had only a few bucks in my pocket, even when I ate no food for a day, I felt things only people living their lives feel.

Joy, sadness.

Pleasure, disappointment.

Excitement, fear.

Loneliness, hope.

Failure, success.

Since I became successful, I stopped feeling these things. I stopped facing real life.

Real life situations.

How could I ... be locked, hidden in the warmth of the home before the real world out there, around me.

Just like in the Bronx, where I was only locked in my parents' apartment just in front of the television – now in Los Angeles, just locked in the house with Sara, living only for work and television. I have always had the opportunity to stand up, to move further and to come out into the real world, among real human beings. Instead, I lied at home, sitting in one place far from the real world of real human beings.

Gifted with exceptional talent, living my ordinary life.

I did not regret what kind of guy I was. I regretted the life I had lived so far.

"Outside, there are people without money, dreaming that one day when they were rich, they would start living a real

life, buy a big house by the ocean, buy the fastest car of the world, travel the world, meet the most famous personalities – that they would tell their own story to the whole world, doing what they want, when they want. You do not have to dream about that fairy tale life, Tom, you have to live that life. You have everything you need to do so."

"Have you succeeded?"

"Yes,"

"Do you have more money than you need?"

"Yes."

"Are you convinced you can reach more than just this? That you deserve more than just this?"

"Yes."

"Are you happy with your life so far?"

"No!"

"Are you convinced that you have fulfilled your potential?"

"No!"

"Are you determined to do something about your life?"

"Yes"

"So do it!!!

Go out. Travel.
   Encounter new people.
   Share your success with others.

Go for some adventure, danger.
Fulfill your potential.
Overcome your limits, your fears.
Leave behind some legacy.
You must celebrate your wins, not hide them inside you where they will be forgotten.

In your life, you have achieved great things, remarkable successes, yet you live your life like some stupid window cleaner getting minimum wage.
When will you start to enjoy your life?
How much money do you have to see in your bank account so you can go and enjoy your life?
In your 60s? When will you have 30 million dollars in your bank account?
Wake up!
In your 60s, you won't be able to walk 10 feet without needing to stop. You may not reach your 60th birthday, so what then?
If you die tomorrow, would you die as somebody who used his life to the fullest? As somebody who fulfilled all his dreams? Hmm, can you say that honestly to yourself? Finally, I am going to the place where I can rest? Did I do everything I ever dreamt of? Did I say everything I ever wanted to say? Have I visited all the places I ever wanted to visit? Hmm?
Because I do!
If at the moment some fucking terrorists shot me outside, I would die with a good feeling, in a good mood, that the time I got I used the best I knew how.
I would die happy, with no regrets.
Think about it, Tom!"

I did not ask any more questions that day. I had a lot more than I needed. With crazy thoughts, I came back home, where Sara was already cooking dinner.

Spaghetti with chicken. After a very long time, she had come home from work in a good mood, with energy, with the power of doing something. Something that had nothing in common with lying on the couch, the bed, or with her work. Smiling, she asked me how my day was. I told her about the big changes in my studio. How I hired three employees to work for me full time. That I changed the name of my studio to TS aDesign Inc.

How I decided to change my attitude towards life. And, of course, how Marion invited us to his party, this time not at his luxury mansion, but at the club Ghost.

She looked at me with a strange look as if she did not understand what I was trying to say. She looked at me with misunderstanding. I suggested that she take a break from work for a couple of weeks. We could go together somewhere, to an exotic island, to Fiji, or to the Bahamas. To enjoy some adventure and, above all, to leave that boring stereotype which had been imprisoning us for years.

Same bullshit as the last time. From her mouth, it was the same bullshit as before! That now she has to work harder than ever before. Otherwise, she may get stuck and not promoted. *"When they promote me, Tom, I promise we'll get out of here together and go on the most expensive and most exciting vacation of our lives. Just wait, honey, just wait…"*

As a good partner and fiancé, I kept my opinion to myself. I knew that I would not reach anything by fighting. Only an argument. She tried her best to make me happy by putting together a romantic dinner in our kitchen, and at the end of the night walking together on the beach. Under the shining stars.

I enjoyed it.

We both enjoyed it.

That evening I felt amazing. She even agreed to the party we were supposed to attend.

The next morning, however, everything came rushing back. All my feelings, desires, plans, dreams. I knew the only way to shut them up was to fulfill them. To actually do them. I could not wait for Sara's promotion. I know it sounds horrible, but Sara had been working for nearly two years on this promotion of hers, and she's been saying the same thing the whole time: *"they will promote me next week. They will promote me next month. They will promote me next year."*

This was the same month after month, year after year.

I could not wait any longer.

No way!

I did an unacceptable thing for me. I went out to the shopping mall. I wasn't thinking about doing some random food shopping or visiting the art supply store. My desire brought me straight to the Ferrari dealer.

Yes.

I was there to buy a good car, especially a fast car. I was bored with my old Toyota. I was bored by being invisible.

I got a taxi to the shop, I left the Toyota in front of my house with a sign in the back window: for sale. I realized one interesting thing at the Ferrari dealer, not known for me before. The level of the salesperson raises with the price of the car you'd like to buy. Just when I entered the store, I got the best cup of coffee I ever drank. I did not say which model I wanted to buy, or what I'm actually aiming at, and I already had the attention of all the people who were there. An older man in a blue suit explained to me everything about each model.

I could sit down, try it out – and man, it's a wonderful experience to sit behind the wheel of one of the most expensive and fastest supercars in the world. Everyone was treating me like I was some honored man. I thought I was going to buy them all. But one Ferrari had to be enough in the beginning. I tell you, when I paid such a high amount for the 488 GTB model with my credit card, my head started to shake from nervousness.

I never spent so much for anything that I had to use alone. Then I remembered the fact that I had to pass through all those obstacles I had to deal with just to stand there. A headache was replaced with a big smile on my face. A minute later I was sitting in my new Ferrari 488 GTB in red. I thought I was in the cockpit of a jet.

When I started the engine, I did not hear any sound, just the sweet melody my ears were listening to. The gas pedal on the floor was causing shivers to go all over my body. My body was full of adrenaline. It was an unbelievable feeling to drive such a beautiful, powerful super fast car. I know how Brian O'Conner felt when he was driving his Nissan Skyline GT-R.

I didn't see the limitations on the streets. It would be a sin not to cross the speed limit with such a car. Every single girl near the road I was passing looked over at me.

At that moment, I remembered Connor McGregor driving his black SUV saying: *Every time people say: spend your money on an experience rather than on material things. Well, fuck that! This for me is an experience and also it is material. So I killed two birds with one stone.*

I agreed with him. I felt driving my old Toyota had been like driving a golf cart.

"How did Sarah feel when you went to pick her up at her work in your Ferrari?"

I did not go to pick her up that day. There was no reason to do so. Sara never liked cars. She literally hated them, because of the pollution, or whatever.

Directly from the store I went to Marion. To the guy who changed my life. Finally, I was able to ride down Hollywood Boulevard without any shame on my face. I felt exactly as I had during those times when I earned my money by working in the kitchen, and I bought my first brand sneakers. At that time I felt like the king of the streets. Now I also felt like the king of the streets. I came to Marion without any warning. I wanted to surprise him with my new, noisy red toy. He and his friends welcomed me with great applause. I'm sure, if I told him to do so, he would be rolling out the red carpet to welcome me. They were happy together with me.

They invited me to join some supercar owners club.

I took everyone for a ride out on the streets.

If you would have called me a week ago to ask me what I would be doing today, my answer would be nothing unusual. I would be sitting behind a desk in my studio and a designing skyscraper.

Now if you called me wondering what I was really doing, I would like to answer: I'm driving my red Ferrari at breakneck speeds on the streets of Los Angles with a sexy brunette on the passenger seat. My new car had made an impression on them.

No jealousy. Just admiration!

"Having such a supercar is just the starting point! Now's the time to take care of the owner of that supercar. As the owner of a Ferrari you have to dress the part. Not like a Ferrari mechanic," Marion said.

"You're right!" I answered. "I gotta buy some new clothes. Can you recommend me some of those fancy outlet stores?"

"Of course! Not only do I share them, but I'm also planning to visit them right now. I have to buy some new watch and shoes. Let's get some lunch first. Then we'll go shopping. Agreed?"

"Sure!"

everly Hills. A place filled with luxury, wealth, and stars. The place had not been revealed to me yet. I thought I was right there in the capital of millionaires. No common cars driving the roads or parked near the road.

No homeless people picking around dumpsters.

No dirt or trash on the pavement.

No cheap Chinese restaurants that I could eat in, the same as in my neighborhood.

"Can I recommend our Italian summer truffles, and for dessert a chocolate cupcake with gold leaf?" our waiter asked me politely.

"Great choice, sir! Serve it, please" I confidently responded to him even when I did not have a clue how much would it cost or how would it taste. Actually, no guest at the restaurant had any idea how much they have to pay until the moment we got the bill because the menu did not contain any prices.

While we were waiting for our food, Marion asked me if I would come on Friday together with Sara to his party.

My answer made him totally happy. But then there was a question that did not make me feel so well. He wondered out loud where and when I would go for a holiday with Sara.

Disappointed, I explained to him the reason for our postponement of what was better called my adventure. After a moment of silence, he said to me: *"Tom, you are a young and as well adult man! All your life is ahead of you. If you are going to approach your life this way, you will have all your life over too soon. Don't let anyone tell you what, when and how to do it. You, Tom, you know what's best for you. Trust me, I know how it feels when the people you love, people who should be your support, are your brakes and barriers."*

The conversation was interrupted by the pleasant voice of the waiter. *"Sir, your main dish Italian summer truffles, and a chocolate cupcake with gold leaf as dessert. Bon appetite."*

Every bite tasted like a paradise garden. I had never tasted food like this in my life and the desert, I thought, would have gold that was tasteless.

I was wrong.

The gold tasted delicious and so luxurious.

With a full belly and happy taste buds, we moved out, to all the luxury boutiques with their luxury goods. Marion took me to his most profitable business.

To Louis Vuitton.

The young salesperson greeted him gently and hugged him. They knew each other personally. Then, the lady greeted me as well and asked me what I'd like to take ho*me*. "*Everyth*ing" Marion answered instead of me.

So I let him choose the clothes. We had the same style. We were passionate about the same things. I knew I could trust him. Usually, when Sara asked me to join her for shopping, I wished for traffic jams, bad weather, or a problem with the tires. I just wished for anything that could stop me from shopping with Sara. I hated it. She considered it a pleasure, I took it as punishment.

In that store with Marion, the situation changed. I could imagine spending at that shop all day. I fell in love with that place. I fell in love with those things. I fell in love with the atmosphere. Generally, I did not feel like I was in a shop. We sat in chairs, we sipped some coffee, we talked to the sales assistants, and Marion showed me some of the clothes.

No stress. No pressure. No rush.

There was no unpleasant smell of clothes reminding me of a Chinese factory.

No unpleasant sales assistants.

No cheapness.

No crowds of people.

In the beginning, when I entered the store, I was shocked. Why did an ordinary black t-shirt with a small white label cost 300 dollars her, when in Walmart I recently saw the same t-shirt without the small white label for 7 dollars? After a few minutes, I found out why so many people are willing to pay all that money for a luxurious outfit. It's simply not comparable to shopping in cheap stores. Not only did I feel better, more comfortable, more important in my new Louis Vuitton brand, but I also looked much better in it.

I did not leave that shop with my old clothes, in the cheap clothing I had been wearing since that morning. I put my old clothes in the place where they belonged.

Into the smelly trashcan.

My body covered in Italian clothes, Marion introduced me to another store across the street. No clothes or accessories to sell. In that shop, they presented masterpieces.

Rolex watches and the brand Patek Philippe.

Several pieces cost more than my new Ferrari. The shopkeeper also knew Marion personally. I had a feeling that everyone in Beverly Hills knew Marion personally. Up to then I was okay with my 16 dollar Casio watch. It was enough. It did what it had to do. It showed the time. I didn't ask for anything more. The watches in that store showed more than just the time. Success.

Wealth.

Power.

Prestige.

Everything was symbolized by those watches.

Wearing them on your wrist meant one thing:

this is not a normal guy.

And I'm not a normal guy!

I bought my first Rolex sky-dweller watch. I thought I would look like an idiot if I had nice luxury suits, a Ferrari in the garage, and a cheap plastic Casio watch. While I spent almost $35,000 for my watch, Marion spent nearly $200,000 on a Philippe Patek watch. I did not leave again with the same watch as I had earlier that morning. I put it where it belonged.

Into the trash. Just like my clothes.

With a golden Rolex on my wrist, shining like a Christmas candle on the Christmas tree, we visited the third store. Marion's personal tailor Pierre.

One blue suit for everyday use, one black suit for social events. I just wanted one blue suit only, but I did not know what to wear to that party, so I even allowed myself to get some kind of other suit.

Extra costs, extra service.

Tailor-made Italian suits in less than 1 hour.

Crazy, right?

On that day, I pleased myself a lot. The most important woman in my life, Sara, was not excluded.

I bought her a great diamond necklace.

The dream of every woman living on this planet. All those glossy shopping bags full of expensive stuff fit neatly into the trunk of the car. Driving a supercar through the streets of sunny Los Angeles, listening to the most favorite song of my heart: Jeremih – Imma Star.

I thought I told ya Imma a star

You see that ice

You see the cars

Flashy lights everywhere we are oh oh

Livin' life, there's no tomorrow

I thought I told you I'm a star

You see the ice?

You see the cars

Flashy lights everywhere we are oh oh

Livin' life, there's no tomorrow

I got money I don't need a range

I'm a pimp I don't need a cane

Big deals charlie you can keep the change

Now that I got the torch Imma gonna keep the flame

Imma keep my aim gotta make the big shots

In my latest suit Louvie V flip flops

Got a bad bitch her hair 'n' nails tip top

Jeremih got the game on the slipknot

Just before the stacks I got rubber bands

Consumers only want you to supply demand

So here I am check my DNA

Gettin money is the only thing on my resume

…

Back home, I had to solve out one important point. My old car.

I found three messages on my message machine. Every one of them was from potential buyers of my old, useless Toyota. Finally my Ferrari could stand proudly in front of my house. Not an old wreck. Shortly after a phone call from those interested in the car, I invited one of them to my home. In 20 minutes, he honked in front of the house. The buyer looked excited.

"I'll give this car to my son for his 18th *birthday"* he told me.

I congratulated him, praised him for being a great father and praised his son for having this father. In my head, I thought the exact opposite. What kind of father is this, buying such a wreck for your own son on his 18th birthday?

He will be laughed at by all his classmates.

When I have a son, on his 18th birthday, I'll buy him a yacht and not an old car meant for grandmas.

Not only did I get $7,000 in cash for that wreck, but I also got a new parking space in front of the garage. Finally, I was able to park my Ferrari in the right place. No one in the neighborhood owned a car like me. Nobody!

While the red gem was shining outside the house, its owner was fighting inside the house. I squeezed the new clothes into a small, modest closet. The smell of luxury was flowing all over the house. Out of curiosity, I started to count. I needed to know how many dollars I spent on shopping. Let me tell you, that sum had many zeroes at the end. I spent almost $300,000 in one day.

From my bank account, a large amount of money disappeared that I had saved for years. During my accounting lesson Sara came to the house with a lot of questions about the car parked in front of our garage.

Women always expect long answers to their questions. I did not met those expectations.

I answered briefly, but with a short sentence: a reward for my hard work, my dear!

I answered badly. I've never seen her so angry or screaming during the time we've been living together. Her face turned red. She must have been so angry herself because her veins on her body looked as if she just done some heavy lifting at the gym.

In my head, I was looking for an explanation of her rude behavior.

What have I done wrong?

What did I say wrong?

Then I remembered. I had to do something I forgot to do. You're stupid. It finally crossed my mind.

The diamond necklace, how could I have forgotten. I took it out from one of the many glossy shopping bags, and with the words "Sorry Sara, I almost forgot, this is for you," I handed her a brown leather box with the diamond necklace in it.

I'm sure that the screaming was replaced with a sweet kiss, right?

I wish you were right. I wish you were right. That necklace just made everything worse. A normal woman would love a guy who was also buying a diamond necklace for her, but my future wife Sara wasn't one of those ordinary women. Instead of thanking me, I received a slap on my cheek.

How could you be so naive?

Why did you buy me something I did not ask you for?

How could you be so selfish?

Who gave you permission to spend our money without my approval.

While I'm working on my promotion at work, you're running around to stores where you are spending our money on such stupid and unnecessary things like a little kid.

I was not interested in arguing with her. I never was, until she emphasized the words "our money."

"What?

Our money?

What do you mean, Sara, our money?" I screamed back.

"You spend all of your hard-earned money buying company shares where you work because you naively believe that it will help you get your promotion.

I pay all the bills, food, shopping.

You live on my money.

It's you, Sara, dependent on my hard-earned cash.

It's you, Sara, who should be grateful for everything I do for you, for us.

And now when I like to use my money and spend it a bit by myself, you tell me how selfish I am? Hmm.

I've never really done anything in my life for myself. I've lived under my own level when I did not have to.

So please do not tell me that I'm selfish!"

Can you imagine what came next? She kicked me out of the house. Sara kicked me out of my own house, bought with my own money.

Unbelievable.

Where did you go? Or what did you do?

I took the car keys and I left. I called Marion asking if I could sleep at the mansion. Of course, he agreed. Thank god he agreed. He just excused himself that he would not be able to personally talk to me because he was shooting an ad campaign in Monaco. I did not take it tragically. I had a place to sleep. And if I were to be honest, solitude would only good be for me. Get rid of all these demons in my head, in my mind.

Leave only one voice, the one that is the most important. My own inner voice.

His housekeeper prepared a room for me, she made the evening meal, she has asked me if I would have a company tonight. "No! Of course not!"

I answered her.

Late that night, I found out why the servant had asked me. At 11 she entered my temporary room, a young brunette with such a perfect body, so beautiful.

Just looking great.

She did not want to play chess with me or play Destiny 2. Marion sent her to me with one goal only. Get the anger out of my head. To be more accurate, the brunette put a question mark in my head.

I resisted her perfect body seen only in her underwear, her perfect face with big eyes.

It helped me. It helped me realize the mistake I made.

No touching.

No words.

No funny business.

On my way home I bought a bottle of red wine together with a bouquet of red roses.

I saw the lights on in my home from the road. I found her lying flat on the couch crying. I had to make right what I had done wrong. Okay, I went to her, and I honestly apologized. She did the same.

She apologized for her words, for her behavior.

S ome people are afraid of tears.
Some people are ashamed of their tears.
I thank god for my tears.
The tears helped me remove those invisible demons from my head, from my mind, from my body.
In nature, when heaven cries, plants grow.
Usually when people cry, they lose something.

Two days later, on the day of Marion's birthday party at Sunset Blvd, a developer called me from London. He very much admired my skyscraper designs, so he decided to hire me to design one of the world's tallest skyscrapers. He had one condition.

The whole process for the design had to be carried out under his control in London, such a long distance away. I was given the opportunity not only to travel, but also to work. To spend some money and also earn some money.

I could not refuse such an offer. Right after the end of the call from the developer, I booked the most expensive room in a hotel right in the center of London. A first class flight was also booked of course. I checked with my guys in the studio. They were working hard, disciplined, without any reluctance. I had a great feeling with them. I had a great feeling with myself. I have been forced to let strange people do my work.

I always thought only I was able to do my best work, no one else.

Let me tell you, when I was standing over them watching their designs take shape, I had to admit in my mind that such elaborate, detailed and great designs I would not even design by myself.

They not only saved me time – they have done well with my business.

I left for the ladies' boutique to pick up a party dress for Sara. From the boutique, I headed to Ghost club without any stops, where Marion needed some help to prepare his party. As I was expecting, he welcomed me with the question:

"How did you enjoy Monica, in the guest room?"

"For my eyes it was wonderful, for my heart not sufficient." That was my answer.

He knew Sara had something to do with it. That's why he warned me not to let someone else influence me. I nodded my head.

The conversation about Monika and Sara ended. Fortunately.

Shortly before 9, I was in a terrible state. Sara had been in the bathroom for more than two hours. Quite an amount of time for someone who did not even want in the beginning to go. Then when she finally came out, I nearly lost my mind. She looked like a princess in that blue dress. Incredibly beautiful. In the time that we've been a couple, we did not have much of a chance to attend social events together. Probably the party was the first event we were going to together.

The first time Sara sat in the passenger seat in my Ferrari. The first time she stood by my side in a nightclub. Sara had to admit that to go out, it was a good idea.

How did you manage to convince her to go to that party?

I used precise words. I told her if she did not feel well there, or if she gets tired, we'll come home immediately.

A fair agreement, for the both of us.

Together with Sara, we congratulated Marion on his 29th birthday. We gave him his birthday gift. He did not even expect this gift, not in his wildest dreams. A finished draft of his megayacht.

It took me less than two weeks.

His sincere hugs were worth more than everything.

I was very keen on our friendship.

He had brought some light into my life wrapped in darkness.

Great music, great drinks, great people, great entertainment – a great place.

We enjoyed it there.

Not only me but also Sara.

When she wasn't dancing on the dance floor with me, she was chatting with her new friends. She looked happy. Only her cup filled with orange juice made a little stir among the other party guests. Every time I checked, I did not notice any anger in her green eyes.

The VIP section was full of large creatures. NBA and NFL stars, models, bloggers, rappers, entrepreneurs. As soon as Marion showed his draft of his megayacht to the businessmen sipping champagne from golden glossy bottles, I got the invitation to join them.

They gave me a good impression. When I joined a group of Japanese businessmen, I was very pleased with their words of praise and acknowledgment. They gave me their admiration. The guests, no not matter whether man or woman, were all people my age.Young people with their whole lives ahead of them. Such young people, yet still so successful. Not only had they succeeded, but they were the same age as me.

At lunch as I helped Marion prepare the party, he told me something about every guest. I wasn't the only one who had to go through hell to get where I got and to live the life I wanted. A lifetime of struggles that we had spent all our time fighting just to overcome. These Japanese businessmen owned working spaces throughout all of Asia. With huge amounts of enthusiasm, they shared their bizarre business plans: to create the largest workspace in Tokyo.

They had the courage, money, and vision. Only one thing was missing: an architect to suit their tastes. An architect with a wealth of experience.

An architect with the courage to design it.

I knew one architect with such a wealth of experience and the courage to bring their plans to life – and that architect was sitting directly in front of them. Those times of silence and modesty were over.

I began to talk about myself, my clients, my company, my employees, and all the buildings I designed.

They listened to me the whole time with full attention. And one minute later, we made a deal.

My company would design the largest workspace in all of Asia. In such a short time, I had received two big international orders. Not only that. I would be able to travel even while I was working.

One week in London, one week in Tokyo. Altogether two weeks away from Los Angeles, amazing!

With this good news in hand, I went to see Sara. I couldn't find her the last place she had been seen with her new friends.

The same group of girls were in the same place, only one member was missing: Sara. I asked them where I could find Sara.

None of them knew.

I thought she might in the bathroom, so I just stood around waiting at the entrance to the lady's room. But I didn't manage to find her there. I ran all over the club, but I couldn't find her anywhere. I was scared for her. In all that noise, I would never have a chance to hear my phone ringing, so I ran outside of the club for a bit and called Sara. All of a sudden, I found out where she was. She didn't even have to tell me – the sound of her ringing phone revealed her location.

She stood on the corner of the street, waiting for a taxi home. I did not have the opportunity to share the news with her before she started spitting out her anger at me. She was giving off a very negative vibration and really bad energy.

"How can stand the company of these people? How can you even want to spend time with them?" she screamed like crazy.

The people around us were all looking at us.

"What's going on, babe?" I asked her.

"Every single person in the club only cares about enjoying life. This isn't us. We aren't like them, Tom! We are not the same as them. We do not need to live our lives like them. The city, our house, our work, we have everything we need.

Nothing more.

I'm not interested in staying any longer, I leaving for home with or without you."

Usually, under normal circumstances, I would have gone with her. And I would have gone home with her, but Sara wanted to leave less than an hour from the start of Marion's birthday party. Of course, I couldn't go so early. The party hadn't even gotten started.

Oh my God, I thought.

She may have done it on purpose. The recently forgotten argument was repeating itself again. Sara hurried back home in a taxi, while I returned back to the club.

The joy of enjoying my life was gone.

Only anger and limitations was what this woman was adding to my life.

Several shots of vodka helped me to forget the argument from just a few minutes ago. I drank more of the vodka, watching the bottle grow emptier and emptier.

The more shots of vodka in me, the more I felt the desire for another woman, and it was uncontrollable. I had lost out on the opportunity before.

This time, I was determined not to repeat it.

The girl who was sitting close to me in my Ferrari on the day I bought it attracted me the most.

I saw her dancing on the dance floor Beyoncé.

She gave off an enormous, positive energy.

She looked so beautiful.

I wanted her so much.

Without a bad conscience, I approached her and started dancing with her.

Touching my sweaty body, she brought me to the dark side.

She knew how to have fun. Not like Sara.

Tender touches, passionate kisses.

More tender touches and passionate kisses. From the dance floor straight to Lara's apartment.

I spent a wonderful night in the company of a gorgeous girl.

I cheated on my fiancé, Sara? Yes!

Did I regret it? No!

For the first time since I started my relationship with Sara, I woke up in the morning lying close to another woman.

"Why did you cheat on Sara? The woman you loved, the woman who loved you."

A loving woman should be your support, someone who supports you in anything.

A loving woman should be the person that will listen to you, she'll help you.

I did not feel that during the last few months, she was doing what a loving women was supposed to do.

The only thing she did was try to discourage me from my plans, desires, and dreams. She was pulling me further down than she was lifting me up.

We both have the right to enjoy our lives.

To celebrate our success, our lives.

I chose to celebrate life, while she chose to delay her life.

The next day I came home for lunch. To Sara, I only said "hello." Nothing more. I took a shower, packed my clothes in my suitcase, and put on my blue suit. About 30 minutes later, I was waiting in the international terminal at LAX.

My flight to London was boarding in 15 minutes. It didn't matter to me. Nothing could take the smile from my face. Nothing! No one could take the smile off my face.

Nobody!

I used the time well. I called the hotel in London, where I had booked a room, to tell them that I would be arriving earlier. I'll need the room for the weekend. No problem to arrange it. In addition to the early arrival, I requested another change. I would not be alone in the room. I would have a guest, Lara.

If you think she was one of those cheap sluts only with the intention of getting to my money, then you are wrong. Lara was a young, self-confident woman.

The independent type, an independent girl with her own success.

She did not need my money.

As a model, she could afford anything.

Everything she laid her eyes on.

Only her heart could not have everything.

My arrival into her life filled a place in her heart. Even though had not spent a single day together, I had the feeling that I knew her my whole life. We spent the entire week visiting luxury shops, restaurants, nightclubs, and in bed.

No stress. No worries. No work.

Only pleasure. Huge amounts of pleasure. Visiting this new country brought entirely new thoughts into my mind.

On Monday morning, after a weekend full of excitement and new experiences, I began to deal with business matters, only business.

A black limousine belonging to the London developer picked me up right from the hotel and brought me to my client's office. It looked amazing, or as he said, "so green and also so genius and uniquely positive."

After a short excursion around the office and after a briefing with his team, I got to work. In spite of the developer's ideas, I wanted to draw the design myself.

I was just following my intuition and imagination.

A noise from the nearby construction site interrupted me a little, but I did not let myself get too distracted. Later, after an hour of sitting at the table almost without moving an inch, I introduced my suggestion for the skyscraper. As usual, I exceeded all expectations. My draft was approved by the developer together with his team of 21 architects. I immediately returned to the hotel where I started to draw.

It was clear that I could not draw a whole skyscraper in just the week that I had to spend in London. In the US, it took me two months – in the UK, it would also take me two months.

I had to do something, and I had to do it quickly.

Really quickly.

In such a beautiful city, I did not want to be locked for all those days in a luxurious hotel with a pencil in hand. I could have stayed in my studio in Los Angeles doing the same thing, and I would have even saved the thousand dollars I paid for one night at that hotel. I asked Lara about what she would recommend. Her advice was exciting, but also scary.

"Find some people to do it for you." That was her advice.

But before I could do it, I needed the opinion of a single person. Marion.

I called him from the balcony of the hotel room. He agreed with Lara. He would do that in my place as well. I did not need much more convincing.

There was only one problem: finding the right people.

I did not have a clue where to find an exceptional architect in London. Luckily the Internet and intuition gave me a helping hand.

During my stay with Mr. Morris, I had a chance to work with one of the guys who had come from Manchester.

I had already added him to my network of contacts on LinkedIn.

Jackpot!

His status contained the best news: open to new opportunities.

I had found the right person I could believe in and wrote him without delay:

Hi Garrett, I have a great deal of interest for you, if you are convinced that you want to build something big in your country, call me ...

Later that night, I woke up the sound of my phone buzzing. The bad weather in London had only one advantage: when you went to bed, from the moment your head hit the pillow you'd be asleep like a log right up to the painful sound of your alarm clock. All that rain would make even bats sleepy.

"Who was calling you so late at night?"

Opportunity.

Garrett had accepted my challenge.

He dared to take advantage of the opportunity. Actually, he wanted to do more than just use it. He wanted to know all the details about my plans, how he could bring success to life. I knew if I put down the phone that night without explaining all the details, I wouldn't be able to get back to sleep. Actually, my thoughts would eat me alive.

In the middle of the night, with the cold rain pouring outside, I arrived at a restaurant five minutes away from the hotel. I was lucky. Garrett had some free time while he was in London. Otherwise, I would not have had the chance to meet him in person. I told him my big plans over some tea. And I surprised him. He thought I wanted him to work for me as an external architect in London. It would too much of waste of time to let him just draw for the whole day. So I introduced the great plan I had in mind for him.

Many great ideas.

I offered him the position of director of the new London branch of my architect firm. He needed some time to think, and I could he was worried whether he would manage. *"I have never done anything except for drawings and blueprints,"* he told me.

"You're right, Garrett, so it's time for you to learn something new," I assured him. "

You are a born leader, you are a director.

I believe in you.

I know you and your skills.

Together we can achieve great things."

I did not give him any space to think.

Instead, I gave him the space to grow.

He did not disappoint me. I knew he was the right one.

Garrett ultimately agreed.

He seized the opportunity.

From the restaurant, we moved back to my room at the hotel. We had to. The restaurants were all closing. In my room, we were looking for appropriate, and especially exclusive, spaces to open my branch. I knew the price would be very high and the range of options would be very low. In London, the best places to rent are already claimed for hundreds of years in advance.

As a compromise, we found what we were looking for.

A large space to rent near a Selfridges.

Due to all this excitement we completely lost track of the time. The real estate broker representing the owners of the rented premises reminded us that I was calling him around 3 o'clock in the morning.

Of course he was sleeping in his warm bed, and I had woken him up.

Thank God I hadn't called an hour ago to a normal real estate broker. The phone was answered up by an extraordinary broker, obsessed with success and money. Not only did he enjoy my interest, but he also invited me to see these spaces not the next morning at 8 o'clock.

Not over lunch at noon.

Not at 8 at night.

This broker invited me to see it right away:

at 3 in the morning on a chilly, rainy day!

Unbelievable. Crazy.

We took a taxi and arrived at Duke Street around 3:15. All the buildings around had their lights out.

Except for one. The site met all my wildest dreams. The space overcame all my strict requirements. The views from the window, availability, size, security. In my head I already imagined my staff working there on remarkable buildings of worldwide admiration.

At a time where 99 percent of London residents were sleeping silently in their warm, comfortable beds, I had found the space for my first branch in Europe. The rent was signed and paid for 10 years in advance. The real estate broker left the premises, but we did not.

Sitting on the bare floor surrounded by empty white walls, we got back to work. I was looking for a designer for the branch office space, while Garrett called architects to offer them a job. Everything we ready by sunrise. With dark circles under my eyes, I left for a meeting with a strongly recommend interior designer. Garrett also departed to meet our new employees. Right after we met, the designer started to get to work. I did not have a lot of time, but I had a lot of money. This helped me speed up the whole process of turning nothing into something.

Through my phone, I set up my own company: TS aDesign LTD.

A company with six employees. Garrett as the director and five architects with so much experience.

A modest start, but great ambitions.

Without any break or rest, I carried on. I notified the developer about some minor changes. Of course, I assured him that there would be no impact on his project and nothing would ruin his plans. He accepted it with a sense of understanding.

He admired my courage and my ambition to widen my team outside the United States.

And though I would not be working on the design of his skyscraper anymore, I would still be supervising it.

I thought it would be great from my side to celebrate this great step with other people by side, not just alone as usual. So I booked some stylish VIP tables in a luxurious nightclub, where I invited Garrett, the new staff and the developer's entire team.

Everybody immediately accepted my invitation. Outside the office gather a bunch of people in suits, normally living a completely different life. All that seriousness, arrogance, supremacy, workaholism were set aside for a while. That night I met many influential people.

Entrepreneurs.

Athletes.

Politicians.

That night, I even met Marion's inspiration, Watchanish, in person.

When I was just a slave to my own studio, I was barely connected with 40 people on LinkedIn.

Since I became the owner of my own international architectural company, I grew to more than 500 connections on LinkedIn. If I had continued to work by myself between the four walls of my studio, I would never have succeeded in achieving what I achieved.

I spent the rest of my stay visiting galleries, museums, restaurants, and nightclubs. I do not remember a day without any rain.

Such terrible weather in such an amazing country. Shortly before I left for home, I stopped by the branch. That interior designer had done truly remarkable work. We still only had one client so far.

One client.

I knew if I wanted to jump in London, I would need big orders from big-name clients. I gave clear instructions to Garrett: invite every important developer in town to lunch. Agree with them on some form of cooperation and if necessary hire other architects.

Get started right away.

Right now!

The money that I spent the week before in Beverly Hills on shopping, in London I invested in the growth of my company, while back in Los Angeles I had my company consisting of three employees, my own house, a Ferrari, Rolex watches, tailor-made Italian suits, luxury clothing, girls – now supplemented by the branch of my company in London with six employees, a new black American Express card, influential friends, and endless partying.

I had reached it all with hard work and the willingness to take risks. Nothing else had helped me get there.

That's why I stopped meditating, affirming, visualizing.

I found out that all the lessons from meditation, visualization, or affirmation gave me nothing.

It did not bring me anything.

No success, happiness, or wealth.

It only took up my precious time.

When I was sitting with my legs crossed, trying to focus only on my own breath, some guy outside was working hard to his last breath.

I sat on the floor, he was living life.

He took steps forward, while my body stayed motionless in the same place like a tree.

While I was sitting at home in a warm bed with my eyes closed, I imagined my success, wealth, and glory, meanwhile out there, some guy was fighting for his success, wealth, glory, and belongings.

I was sitting in one room for years patiently waiting, so why should I keep on meditating?

To calm myself down?

No way!

I was sitting in one place for a long time!

I needed to bring noise, agitation, and some turmoil to my life!

I promised myself that no longer would I do these activities inevitably for the sake of success.

Why should I?

I did not have to imagine with my closed eyes that I was successful – I was already extraordinary and rich.

It was enough to open my eyes and see it.

I saw it.

The people around me saw it.

I am rich, I am successful, and I am exceptional.

I did not have to repeat these things to myself anymore. The people around me treated me like I was successful, rich, and extraordinary.

Shortly before going back to LA, I received an email. Reading this email changed the direction I was traveling in. I was expected in Tokyo.

The design of the most prominent work space inspired me more than the embarrassment of explaining my mysterious disappearance to Sara.

During the long flight from London to Tokyo, I had a courageous feeling in my head.

What if I opened another branch, this time in Tokyo.

A new country, new people, new clients, new projects, new money.

Before I booked my hotel, before I called my clients, and before I ate my first meal in that country I had already set up my own business in Tokyo.

It required more than just the touch of the screen on my phone, as it had in London. I had to fix it all in person. Face to face.

One hour later, I struggled through the crowded Tokyo streets as the proud CEO of my new Tokyo branch.

Nothing could have messed up the tremendous pride I felt in that moment, like of was king of the world. I could do anything without any problems.

I was flying as high as the stars, waiting for my ride to visit my clients as I looked at vacant spaces for rent.

In comparison with London, the prices were lower and the offer was higher. I agreed to have a couple of visits in the afternoon. Like in London, I informed my clients that I was expanding my business and hiring other employees – I think my courage to take a risk, start a business and open my own branch in a totally different, foreign country made a great impression on them.

They no longer called me a small fish.

Now they looked at me like I was a shark.

I promised that I would oversee the design of their coworking space. I agreed with their terms, and they have agreed with mine. Our meeting took place in a local restaurant. They did not enjoy and expect luxury. Modesty was in their veins.

Lara was sitting on an airplane to Tokyo as I checked open spaces in Tokyo for my new branch. I knew that the design and location must be exclusive. Just like our projects.

Without the knowledge of the Japanese language, I tried to get as much information as possible about the companies in the vicinity of the premises.

The first three spaces did not meet my requirements by a long shot. If I were an inexperienced lawyer offering my affordable services, I might be thinking about renting these places, but my plans did not include anything that would be cheap or ordinary.

Some of the real estate brokers did not come at the agreed times as they promised.

Some brokers canceled the offer.

When it all seemed lost, I had an interview that could change my situation. Some little guy in a white suit standing in front of a large glass building called with somebody he'd asked to prolong the rent.

He looked like a very powerful guy.

He held in his left hand a cane with the golden head of a lion.

This is my chance was the only thought that crossed my mind.

I approached him by saying: "I may be wrong, and maybe not, but I assume the building that we are now standing in front of, and the person who you just called a few seconds ago, just ended your rent.

Am I right?" I asked fearlessly.

"It's the truth! You are right, sir" he answered me in a strong Japanese accent.

"You need to find someone who will make use of your premises and pay rent on time, and I need to find a suitable space for my branch with a great rent.

We're both looking for something.

We both need something.

You can figure out my situation,

I can figure out your situation.

Just let me check out your space, and if it meets my demands, I'll pay you rent for the next 10 years in advance.

In cash!"

The wrinkles of anger were replaced by the wrinkles of a smile spreading across his face.

He agreed with my offer and immediately invited me to check not only his buildings and premises, but he also invited me to lunch at his own home.

I had the opportunity to get to know his great and amazing family.

He dressed very modestly.

If you met him outside on the street, you would not think he was such a rich man.

That is, if you did not pay attention to his cane with the golden lion.

Tadashi's house was different.

Chinese porcelain, marble, seat covers with real crocodile skin, luxury cars. At the table, we all ate as a family. Tadashi, his wife, and three neat daughters. While we were eating sushi, a servant cared for everything else. After a delicious lunch, I moved from the dining room to Tadashi's office.

He told me the story of his adventures in Tanzania, where a group of lions attacked their car with his whole family inside. Everything went well in the end, as his family made it without injuries. Only his leg was injured. This explained his issue when walking, and why the golden head of a lion adorned his cane. The lions had taken his possibility of walking as a healthy man. Then he showed me the killer lions with killer instincts.

But I did not see that in them in the pictures. I had looked the lions directly in their eyes, even touching their bodies and their teeth. Tadashi paid a local native in Tanzania to find the group of lions. Then he shot them. The stuffed bodies were brought home on a private jet. Now they were proudly on display in his office.

I realized that he must be a lover of wild animals. That's why I did not know how he came to the elephant tusks hanging on the wall.

"And what about the premises?"

I looked at those spaces, and let me tell you, I accepted without hesitation. I knew if I were hesitating, someone else would take it. I could not let that happen. The site was exclusive. I needed it. When I paid him for ten years in cash, he looked at me in surprise.

"Paper notes? Still used by somebody? I pay for everything only in bitcoins. You Americans are weird people" he said.

I had my space, I only needed the people to fill them. Now I had the experience on how to do it. I called Garrett back in London. I told him what I had done in Tokyo. Then I asked him for a recommendation for some of the Asian guys who would become a part of the Tokyo branch. In an email, he sent a long list of guys. Of course there was a note: *"Tom, you are either the craziest or the greatest bastard in the world."*

Of course I was the greatest bastard.

It was less than seven hours from my arrival in Tokyo. In that time, I had done a lot of things. Important things for my life, for my future, for my business.

I started to call the names on the long list from Garrett. Many had no interest in following my vision. They did not have anything against me. They just did not like working for someone else. Instead, they'd rather travel all over the world only with their backpacks, like a pilgrim.

As the number of names on the list dwindled, my tension grew. I had promised something to my favorite people. If I did not do what I promised, it would destroy me and everything around me. I had been working so hard on it.

Time was running out.

I had to cut back on my demands for my employees due to this time pressure. Otherwise, I would have the premises of the branch with no employees in them.

The rest of the guys on the list were interested in meeting me.

In other words: the last five guys who were unemployed, needing regular monthly income, these are the ones who wanted to meet me.

Two glasses of whiskey gave me the power to complete an interview with these architects. Without much experience, without work ethics, without self-confidence. Only with education and the desire to earn big money.

What I took before as an inconvenience, I took it now as a favor. Probably I didn't have a choice.

I accepted them with one condition: do everything exactly as I say.

"You already had the employees, who became the CEO?"

Me! I became the director.

Temporarily.

I had learned that it was time to teach other people what I learned myself, what life had taught me.

I became their leader.

Their mentor.

That's what I was doing in Tokyo. I felt like I was in New York. It reminded me of my childhood. In our working premises, there was equipment left by the former tenant that helped me a lot. We could start working right away, without having a long to wait for an interior designer. From a nearby shopping mall I bought six new computers, phones, printers, and energy drinks.

A lot of energy drinks.

Without them, I probably would not have been able to get it done.

The guys had gotten their basic knowledge from school. Everything else was on me.

I had to add another rule very soon.

Rule number two: no phones during working hours.

For a moment, I felt like a teacher standing in front of a blackboard trying to teach something to the children, while the children were watching the latest House of Cards episode on their phones without listening to me.

13 days. 13 crazy days until they learned what they needed to know.

Two weeks after my arrival in Tokyo I had my own company – actually, my own branch office, five employees and only one single order. Garrett was asked to invite all of London's high-profile developers to lunch.

In Tokyo, I did not know anyone except those entrepreneurs who I knew from Marion's party in Los Angeles, which were my only clients in that country.

To change the situation it required more than just sending a request to connect on LinkedIn.

The custom in Asian countries is a personal meeting between business partners. I decided to move things forward. The customs are to be followed, I do not break the rules.

Without calling in advance, I came to Tadashi's home.

Knocking at the door did not work.

Shouting did not work.

Carefully I walked over his vast yard surrounded by a high concrete wall.

A tennis court, heliport, sculptures, live tigers, monkeys in cages.

Too much luxury around, with no presence of guards, dogs, cameras.

The usual worker living in an old rented house had better security than he had.

I looked suspicious.

Like a thief looking at your house.

That's why I quickly returned back to the gate. I'm sure if someone saw me in the neighborhood, they would call the police. I could not risk any problems with the police in a foreign country.

On the way back, I lost my way.

I did not have any clue of the direction ahead of me.

I was so lost that I got a little scared.

"You could end up in prison. Prison!" my inner voice screamed.

In a frenzy, at high speeds, I ran to the high concrete fence. I walked alongside it thinking that it would take me to the gate. I only made it a couple of meters unnoticed. My uninvited entry to private property did not stay unnoticed.

A young Japanese girl in a white swimsuit, sunbathing on a wooden bench close to the swimming pool, saw me. Immediately, she started screaming.

I did not understand what the hell was going on.

I did not know a word in Japanese.

I tried to explain in English that I came to look for Mr. Tadashi.

I am not a thief, thieves do not wear tailor-made Italian suits.

I do not know which word she was really interested in, but it worked. She stopped crying.

She gave me the opportunity to explain what I was doing on their private land before she called the gokudo.

I did not understand the meaning of the word, but I had an idea of what that might mean.

I'm Tom Seed. I came here to look for Mr. Tadashi.

I rent some premises in one of his buildings.

I'm not a thief!

I am an entrepreneur, an architect.

Please do not call anyone.

I do not want to cause you any trouble here.

I came here for help.

"You're Tom Seed?" she asked with a sense of surprise.
*"My father told me about you, about your success.
I imagined you as much older, much fatter, more wrinkles.
I apologize for my screaming.*

*Our family is honored in this country. I'm sorry that
I scared you. And I am lucky that I saw you first.
If someone else would see you, that would be
a problem. A big problem.
I'm Mae.
The daughter of Mr. Tadashi.
Nice to meet you."*

"Why did your father not tell me about you when I went for
lunch at your home with the whole family?"
*"I'm sure he had a reason in mind about why he did not
tell you about me. I'm not just his daughter.*

*I am also his accountant and I look after all his money,
which does not allow me much time to spend with my family."*

So beautiful and yet so ambitious. I liked her.

*"My father has one important meeting in town now, but one
hour later he will come back home. We can get to know each
other over a glass of wine in the meantime. Do you agree?"*

Those 60 minutes spent with Mae went by unbelievably fast.
The more she talked about herself, the more comfortable
I was with her.

She did not act like the typical daughter of a rich father
with an everyday habit of having full shopping bags.

This daughter did not spend her father's money.

She managed it as an accountant.

The discussion with Mae was replaced by a talk with her
father. The influence and sign of this man could be found
all over the city. Two crucial things for my success and the
success of my newly opened branch.

"A man with such success, with such a strong personality as you, is ideal for me. You are a symbol of grandeur. You are an inspiration for the average man. I came here to your mansion, asking for help. I do not know anyone except you. I would be honored if you could introduce me to your friends who are building in this city. I am sure I would be a great companion for them and their business."

"You have big plans, Tom, just like me, just like my friends. Tonight, I'm hosting a charity event at my home. Among the guests, you will find many powerful, wealthy people with the passion for creating large buildings. I will be pleased to introduce you personally with some up of them. Please come tonight, my daughter Mae would also be pleased to see you. Your presence has given my daughter something I have not seen in her eyes for many years.
    Love.
    I would appreciate if you could do one favor for me.
    As a thank you."
    I did what he asked me for with pleasure.

At this charity event, I had to look more than good among all those rich, influential people.

This meant a new tailor-made suit,

shoes,

shirt,

watch,

and a luxury car rental.

It cost me $31,000.

You might think I was a fool to spend so much money on a charity event.

Yes!

A fool would have come in a cheap suit with a cheap plastic watch on their wrist.

I did not spend $31,000.

I invested $31,000.

The first impression is always important.

Everything else is not important.

You have to show off yourself as a successful and ambitious man, that you care for yourself as much as you can.

Because your appearance and your body represents your thoughts and your mind. The fact that I care about myself, that I wear nice, good things, as I say, means that I treat other people like kings.

The suit, watches, shoes, and car for $31,000 could bring me millions in orders from those people.

"Did it work? Did the expensive things help you as expected?"

Of course it worked!

By the way, I got more in terms of charity than I ever expected. Besides establishing some valuable personal relationships with the most prolific Tokyo developers, I won the heart of one girl.

A girl who was scared of me at first.

From the first moment I saw her, I fell in love with her.

I spent a lot of time at this event with her. Actually, I spent a lot of time afterwards with her too. I had such a nice time with her. She showed me how the relationship between man and woman should be – it was perfect. How to support one another, not to destroy one another. To love each other, and not having to hang on to each other. Be one together, not a source of competition.

One month later, my Tokyo branch received 9 bids in total for $2 million. My investment in luxury of $31,000 had brought me $2 million back. This is the stuff you'll never find on YouTube.

Only life can teach you the way.

Completing the design of the biggest coworking space accelerated my success in Asia.

The orders were pouring in like raindrops from the sky. I had to hire new employees and buy new equipment.

We grew incredibly fast.

From the morning to the late evening, every day from Monday to Sunday I was busy.

Meetings with clients.

Lunches with Mae at the restaurant.

Managing my international offices from my office.

Golf.

Shopping.

Driving sports cars through the streets of Tokyo.

In that country, I truly succeeded in business.

All the people who knew me there knew it. I just needed people to know it more. I mean all those unknown people around me.

Buying the latest Lamborghini.

Richard Mille watches and an apartment in Minato-Ku. Dozens of tailor-made Italian suits.

I even started to exercise again. A personal trainer helped me with that. The worst thing in the world is to see a successful young man with expensive clothes on a terrible looking body.

I wanted to look great in the eyes of other people.

I no longer had the same motivation as when I was living in poverty, in the dirt, like in that time I was striving for a better life. Then, I was motivated by my own success. Something to reach for, making money, something to get me away from that dirt, from that poor life.

Now I was motivated to show other people, unknown people around me, how successful I was, how rich I was, how I was extraordinary. How I live in a place surrounded by luxury and wealth.

I once read these wise words in a book: you cannot buy happiness with money.

It's bullshit! Whoever wrote it never had money.

I felt extremely happy. There was no problem

I couldn't through money. None!

And if there are no problems in your life, there are no worries as well.

A life without worries is a good life.

Not just the branch in Tokyo grew incredibly fast. In London, Garrett also made a big move forward. He hired more to his team of what was five architects, adding another 16 experienced architects. This represented twenty-one employees, a branch of more than 50 orders and a turnover of 7 million pounds.

We had accomplished all of this in just 4 months. We weren't a small local player anymore. We started out as a fish in a pond, and we ended up like a big ocean shark. And it all started with one guy who demanded we design his megayacht.

The news of my business's success spread quickly. The most well-known magazines in Asia, as well as in the UK, wrote about me and my success. Interviews on TV almost every day. Everyone asked me the same question: "*how did you manage it so fast?*"

My reply was always the same: "you ask me how I did it so quickly, but I'm asking myself every morning when I get up, why did it take so long?"

Invitations to major events, endless interview requests.
I could choose where and with whom.
I loved it.
I really enjoyed it.
In the US, I was nominated for the Forbes 30 Under 30. As a lost twenty-year-old boy, I remember reading stories in that magazine.
Now people would be able to read my own story in that very same magazine.

When my surroundings started to recognize my success, I started to consider myself successful – I began to feel successful, and I started to feel good.
More than that, it was not only the silent, inner voice in my head that was telling me something.
Now voices, the powerful voices around me, were praising me, telling me that I had reached something,
I meant something.

At the right time, I found a guy who could as a substitute for me. I had all my energy and all my time to enjoy by myself.
Along with Marion and Mae, we all flew to a private island in the Maldives. We spent one month there.
One month filled with pleasure, relaxation, fun, excitement, and adventure.

Diving and swimming in the sea together with turtles, carefree sunbathing on sandy beaches, a quick ride on water scooters, wild parties.

One of the most beautiful periods of my life. Things I was dying to do for a very long time, stuff like skydiving from a plane and bungee jumping, I managed to do. I almost went bungee jumping, to be honest – but my anxiety prevented me from taking the plunge. The whole time Marion was uploading many videos to Instagram. Most got more than 300,000 views in less than 20 hours.

My hard work in the gym had rewarded me with a perfect body. A perfect body admired by thousands of women from all over the world.

During the flight from the Maldives back to Asia, I thought about buying a luxury mansion somewhere near Bel Air. I would live near Marion, it would be amazing.

My best friend and also my neighbor.

It did not take long before my thoughts about my new luxury mansion disappeared. Instead, I had to deal with business matters. I had obviously agreed with everybody that no phone calls would be allowed during my vacation. Obviously, someone forgot to act according to the agreement. Garrett.

He called me even though he did not want to. When I picked up the phone, I could not even think about buying a luxury mansion anymore.

He had bad news for me. Very bad news.

I had to change all my plans, immediately. My staff in Los Angeles had not handed over the designs of the skyscrapers, which were supposed to be handed over more than four weeks ago.

My reputation, my name, was in a bind.

Paid advertising is effective.

Negative advertising from your own clients is ruinous.

It took me a lot of money to fly back to Los Angeles in a private jet. The flight lasted more than 20 hours.

My mind was drowning in toxic thoughts for those 20 hours.

My body busted into a state of cold sweat and fear for more than 20 hours.

More than business, I was worried about a meeting I cared much more about – with my fiancé Sara.

What I would answer if she asked me:

"Where have you been the last five months, Tom?"

"Why didn't you call me at least once?"

"Do you still love me?"

Fortunately, Marion gave me some time.

He offered to let me stay with him in his mansion. It bought me one day.

For one day he helped delay my meeting with Sara.

My head was full of worries, along with an empty stomach also full of worries.

Nothing helped me get rid of those toxic thoughts bouncing around my head.

Not driving my red Ferrari.

Not the gym.

Not even talking.

Nothing worked. Nothing helped me.

Broken down by my own thoughts, I turned to a type of medicine used by many people: a medicine called alcohol. What helped me have fun in the past, helped me not to go crazy.

Early in the morning, with minimal amounts of alcohol in my blood, the worries of yesterday already become part of today.

The sound of my Ferrari so beloved in the past was hated nowadays.

The pain in my head was booming.

Standing in front of the entrance to the premises of my own company, without the ability to enter it.

I could not open the door.

It was locked.

Even though the premises belonged to me, Even when I had the right key from the door,

I could not open those fucking doors.

I knocked. No one opened up.

I shouted. No one showed up.

I rang the bell. Nobody.

I screamed. No one answered.

I didn't get it. At that time, my employees should already be at work as usual.

I felt uncomfortable returning to our house. Five months is long, and I had not visited a single time.

Right after I arrived, an unusual site caught my attention. The garage door was sprayed with graffiti: "Thief!"

"What the hell happened here?" I asked myself.

The front door was unlocked, and the mailbox had been removed.

The beating of my heart was speeding up, the fear of the unknown only making it worse.

I entered my home – literally, only my house.

All the furniture, all the things, all the photos…

they were all gone.

Just the bare walls, the cold floor and my closet filled with luxury clothing.

I checked every room in the whole fucking house. There was almost nothing left there.

What the hell had she done?

I did not understand.

Then, in the kitchen, at the same place where we used to have a massive mahogany table, I found two envelopes.

Two envelopes lying on the ground.

Not advertisements, only problems.

The first envelope was from Sara. She left me a letter saying: "*when two people love each other, there is no reason to cheat. Just remember the moments you spent with me! They will only be memories.*"

The second envelope was from the police: "your company TS aDesign Inc, and you Mr. Seed, are the subject of an international criminal investigation."

Two envelopes,
Two letters,
Two direct shots right into my heart.
My fiancé Sara had left me, and my name and reputation was destroyed.
I did not know what to do.
I did not even know where I was.
I called Marion for help. Immediately I had to get to his home in Bel Air. I got in the car, but I only made it a few feet.
Just a few yards from the house that used to be a home filled with love, police cars with their sirens flashing appeared and blocked the road ahead of me.
I could not do anything. I knew they had come for me. Six cops with their weapons drawn, ready to pull the trigger.
At that moment, I realized how I had destroyed everything.

Broken by the world around me, I was lying handcuffed on the hot pavement.
I had lost everything I ever cared for.
I had lost the most important things that gave sense to my life.
I could go on living further, but I did not have anyone to live for.

Police arrest documents in front of my eyes. Handcuffs on my wrists.
My body sitting in the back of the police car.

My mind melting into a sea filled with regrets.
The sirens screamed on the roof of the police car as tears came streaming down my eyes.

Before I was sent to the judge, I spent eight hours answering some very unpleasant questions in an office room. When I answered all their questions about me, Sara, my business, my clients, Tadashi, and my friends, they brought me to the court in a white van.

In a stroke of bad luck, the very same judge that had seen me thirteen years ago in New York was now deciding my fate in Los Angeles.

He knew me.

I knew him.

"Mr. Seed," he said, "in the past, I gave you the opportunity to learn from your mistakes, to live a life of freedom as a normal citizen of this great country.

Now you stand here again after thirteen years, with the same scrupulous expressions on your face.

Your mom would be proud of you."

Bail in the amount of $100,000 had been paid to save me from having to stay in jail. I only knew one person who had the money to pay.

Marion had saved my freedom.

But our friendship was over.

The magazines that just recently were writing about me as a successful businessman, were now describing me as a criminal. "From successful international businessman to international criminal" – that was the headline in Forbes magazine.

You could find me in all the newspapers, on TV, and everywhere in between. Everyone knew who Tom Seed was. A criminal!

Some journalist wrote an article about my past. How I had stolen that medicine from the pharmacy, how I had stolen food from the mall.

Everything bad from my past blocked out all the good things from my present.

I left court as a free citizen of the United States of America without any respect, worship, or admiration.

No fiancé.

No friends.

No one who could help me.

No one who could embrace or support me.

Only my tailor-made Italian suits.

My house.

My car.

My money.

My bright objects.

Everything else remained trapped in my memories of a glossy past.

The NoMad Hotel, on the corner of Olive Street, provided me with some time to hide away from the outside world. To hide from all the horrible people living in it. In that 5-star hotel, lying in bed between the bed bugs of luxury, I thought about my life.

Everything had started with my work, and it all came to an end because of my work.

At work I got to know Sara, but thanks to work I lost Sara as well.

At work I found my happiness, but thanks to my work I had lost it all.

At work I earned all my money, only to lose all my money through work. I did not have anyone to live for.

I was completely alone.

And that message from Sara… she had decided about everything. I got out of bed and I went out to the balcony, where I undid the metal lock.

For a moment, as I considered to jumping, I heard a voice, saying "don't do it!"

"God doesn't want me to go, God still has plans with me" I thought to myself.

But when I turned around, it was you in the window.
I had not heard the words of God.
I was listening to the words of the hotel's bellboy.

"I don't understand why they called you a villain? Why did they arrest you? You didn't break any laws."
You know, the police told me on the day of my arrest who Tadashi really was. He was the head of the Yakuza in Tokyo. All his possessions, all his money, he had gotten illegally. That's why Mae told me if someone else had caught me sneaking around their yard, I would be in big trouble.
In other words, if I got caught on their land, I would be dead.
Their family earned their respect by killing other people. Their family gained respect due to the slaughter of other people.
Shortly after my arrival in Tokyo, I did not recognize anyone there. Only him.
That's why I came to him and asked him to introduce me to his influential friends. We agreed that I had to do one favor for him – one favor that cost me my reputation, respect, and admiration.

"What kind of favor, Tom?"

To Mae, his daughter, I entrusted the accountancy of my company. She took care of the accounting for my entire international business.
The branches in Tokyo, London, and in Los Angeles, she was in charge. In charge of it all.

Besides managing my money, she did the dirty money laundering, bloody money for her father.

Directly through my business.

When Garrett and the other guys secured large orders from big developers, they immediately started working on them. However, as soon as the clients paid their money, they did not even work on the developers' orders. Mae took most of the money and put it in her family's bank account.

More than 80 clients did not get what they paid for. More than 80 orders not completed.

More than 80 clients are ready to file charges against me.

More than $25 million that Mae had stolen...

That's why people were calling me a villain and a thief.

I was the CEO of TS aDesign Inc, while Mae was an employee of TS aDesign Inc.

I am the one who made the decision. I am the one who the whole world was now blaming.

I fell in with the wrong people.

I opened my heart to the wrong people.

I believed in the wrong people.

I had given everything to the wrong people.

"I can't imagine how you must be feeling, Tom! Your problems are bad, but out in the world, there are millions of people who have much worse problems than you have now.

Some people suffer from hunger or thirst because they have nothing to eat or drink.

Some people suffer from pain because their bodies are sick.

I'm also one of those people with this kind of life. You can't imagine how grateful I would be if I could face the problems in your life.

Two months ago, my wife Genie had a daughter. That same day, God took my beloved wife. The only person I ever had. I grew up in an orphanage.

Without a family.

Without friends.

Just like her.

I did not have time to be sad about her because I had to take care of myself and my little daughter.

From the moment when Genie left me I started working two jobs to afford milk, diapers, and food for my daughter.

No one cared if I had money or if I was healthy.

It was all on me.

While I'm here cleaning the rooms and carrying the leather suitcases of hotel guests, my daughter Katie is down there at reception where my colleague is looking after her.

It's painful to see my little daughter grow up in the hands of a strange woman.

It's painful to see my beloved wife only in pictures.

It's painful to fall asleep every night knowing that if

I lost my work, I would lose my daughter.

And you want to jump from the eighth floor just because you lost your reputation and your good name?

Don't be so stupid!

If you proved yourself that you could get out of the dirt once before, you can do it again.

The heart of one woman, you cannot get back a second time if she is dead already.

Working at this hotel gives me more than just money. This job gives me the opportunity to see rich people living their lives and wealthy people living unimaginable lives.

You wear expensive clothes in which you look great, while your face does not reflect any feelings of happiness.

Your clothes show your success, but your body shows nothing.

Nice packaging, horrible interior.

Outside happy, inside unhappy.

Just like all the rich people living their lives, sleeping in this hotel.

Don't be like them.

Don't be one of them!

Forget about money, things, the opinions of other people. Out there is a woman who is longing for you. Out there – there is a woman that misses you.

Come back inside.

I'm sure your fiancé will forgive you."

"It's not possible. Sara will never forgive me."

"How can you know if you don't try?"

"Because she is pregnant. She does not want to see me again. She wrote it to me in her message."

"Really?

Are you so weak that you'll leave your girlfriend and your child, just like that?

Without a fight?

Go find her and fight to win her back.

You're going to be a father!

Don't be the kind of father who leaves his daughter in the hands of a strange man!

She needs you!

They need you!

He was right.
I still loved Sara, even when I was waking up in the morning in bed with another woman.

Once before, I had left a woman.

The best woman in my life – my mom.

I can't do that again!

I turned back towards the hotel room, taking the first step off the ledge.

But then I suddenly felt the same dizziness I had when I tried bungee jumping in the Maldives.

I lost the strength in my hands and in my legs as there was only darkness growing in front of my eyes.

My body, my paralyzed body, was already falling down.

That person, that bellboy, he didn't see any fear in my eyes as I fell.

He only saw the regret in my eyes.

I would not see my child's first steps.

I would not hear my child's first words.

I would not feel the touch of my child.

I would never watch another movie with Sara in bed.

I would never take a holiday with Sara.

My child would grow up just like me, without a father, without a father to show the way.

Mommy, I can finally tell you how sorry I am...

www.ingramcontent.com/pod-product-compliance
Lightning Source LLC
La Vergne TN
LVHW050657200726
843506LV00010B/1556